Coloring E
about
THE OUR FATHER

Text by MICHAEL GOODE
Illustrations by JOAN S. MINGO

CATHOLIC BOOK PUBLISHING CO.
NEW YORK

GOD'S GIFT: PRAYER

God (Father, Son, and Holy Spirit) has given us the gift of prayer. We can talk to Him as we talk with our parents in a loving way.

(T-696)

NIHIL OBSTAT: Francis J. McAree, S.T.D.
Censor Librorum

IMPRIMATUR: ✠ Patrick J. Sheridan, D.D.
Vicar General, Archdiocese of New York

The Nihil Obstat and Imprimatur are official declarations that a book or pamphlet is free of doctrinal or moral error. No implication is contained therein that those who have granted the Nihil Obstat and Imprimatur agree with the contents, opinions or statements expressed.

We can pray to God at any time and in any place. We can pray
in church, at home, or while walking around.

JESUS PRAYED WHILE ON EARTH

Jesus prayed many times in His earthly life. Before every important moment, He talked lovingly with His heavenly Father.

We can praise God for His goodness, thank Him for His blessings, beg His forgiveness, and ask for His help.

JESUS TAUGHT US TO PRAY WITH FAITH

Jesus taught us to pray with faith. He said: "Everything you pray for will be yours, if you only have faith."

We must always believe that God will answer our prayers in the best way possible.

JESUS TAUGHT US TO PRAY WITH WORKS

Jesus taught us to pray with works. In order to have God hear our prayer, we must do the works that God asks of us.

It is not enough to pray. We must pray and also do good works—like helping older people with their groceries.

JESUS TAUGHT US TO PRAY WITH WORDS

Jesus taught us to pray with words. The disciples asked Him to teach them to pray, and He gave them the words of the Our Father.

"Our Father, Who art in heaven
hallowed be Thy Name.
Thy Kingdom come.
Thy will be done on earth
as it is in heaven.
Give us this day our daily bread;
and forgive us our trespasses
as we forgive those who
trespass against us.
And lead us not into temptation,
but deliver us from evil."

The Our Father is the most beautiful prayer we have. It was given to us by Jesus Himself.

OUR FATHER WHO ART IN HEAVEN. . .

God is our heavenly Father. He made us out of nothing and loves us even more than our parents love us.

OUR FATHER WHO ART IN HEAVEN. . .

We say that God is in heaven. But He is also on earth. He is everywhere, always ready to hear us.

HALLOWED BE THY NAME . . .

We pray that God's Name may be hallowed, that is, given great glory. This takes place when He is known and loved by all.

HALLOWED BE THY NAME . . .

We must do everything for the glory of God. We will then honor
His Name and gain salvation for ourselves.

THY KINGDOM COME . . .

We pray that God's Kingdom may come. His Kingdom will come when God is known, loved, and served on earth.

THY KINGDOM COME . . .

We should let Jesus reign over us as our King in the Sacrament of the Altar and in our hearts.

THY WILL BE DONE ON EARTH
AS IT IS IN HEAVEN . . .

We pray for God's will to be done on earth. God knows what is good for us and always wants that to happen.

THY WILL BE DONE ON EARTH AS IT IS IN HEAVEN . . .

We should always try to do God's will by obeying His Commandments and the Laws of the Church.

GIVE US THIS DAY OUR DAILY BREAD . . .

'We pray that God will give us the good things of each day—especially the meals we share with our family.

We should pray especially for the best thing God gives us each day—Holy Communion. We receive the Body and Blood of Jesus.

We pray that God will forgive us our sins. He is merciful and will forgive us our faults if we are sorry for them.

AND FORGIVE US OUR TRESPASSES . . .

When we do something wrong, we should be sorry for what we have done. Then we should ask God to forgive us in the Sacrament of Penance.

AS WE FORGIVE THOSE WHO TRESPASS AGAINST US . . .

We tell God that we will try to forgive those who have hurt us. For that is what Jesus did on the Cross.

We should always pray that God will help us to forgive those
who hurt us in any way. With His help we can do it.

AND LEAD US NOT INTO TEMPTATION . . .

We pray that God will help us when we are thinking of doing bad things.

AND LEAD US NOT INTO TEMPTATION . . .

We must stay away from the persons, places, and things that lead to sin.

BUT DELIVER US FROM EVIL

We pray that God will watch over our family and protect us from all evil.

We should always ask God's help. He is all-powerful and can protect us from evil of every kind.

PRAYING THE OUR FATHER AT MASS

Every Sunday we pray the Our Father together with all the people at Mass.

PRAYING THE OUR FATHER AT HOME

We should try to say it with special devotion at Mass and at home. For it is the prayer of Jesus.

Thank You, God,
for the Our Father.